life's for living . . . . go live it!

My story depicting true
life experiences in an
abusive relationship

A. FROST

NO LIFE ALOUD!

life's for living . . . . go live it!

ISBN 978-0-9928369-0-0

Cover Design by Chris Sage

Prepared, printed and bound by Allens Printers Limited, Sloper Road, Cardiff CF11 8AB

*My story depicting true
life experiences*

Love and hugs to...

I dedicate this book in memory of my mum.
I hope she is looking down on me with
pride at what I have achieved
since experiencing freedom.

Love and hugs to my gorgeous children
Daniel, Jamie and Ruby.

Eternal love and respect to my dad who
has always stood by me whatever
decision I have made in life.

Love and gratitude to my friends for standing
beside me and for their love and
support throughout.

Index . . .

JUST ME... THEN THERE WERE THREE

HOLIDAY ROMANCE

NO FRIENDS ALLOWED

STAB NIGHT

MY GLASGOW KISS

LITTLE BY LITTLE

LOVE BITES

THE UNFORTUNATE PROPOSAL

MY SPARKLER

MY HEN.... DON'T

WEDDING DAY BLUES

SIGNS

RAMPAGE

PUSH; PUNCH; ANYTIME OF THE MONTH

MY VALENTINE

REMEMBER, REMEMBER THE 5th OF NOVEMBER

I THOUGHT IT WAS ALL OVER... IT IS NOW!

JUST ME... AND THERE ARE STILL THREE

NO LIFE ALOUD!

Introduction

Step inside and allow me to introduce what an abusive relationship looks like from within four walls. I wonder how many of you have been in similar situations and not quite realised at the time that you were being abused? It's hard to recognise abusive behaviour at the time and it's not until we look back that we realise the severity of what was going on.

Wouldn't it be great if we could recognise early in a relationship abusive acts and have both the strength and courage to call it a day and move on to better things. It's just not that easy. We all need help of some description at times. Although we feel we should be able to cope with things life throws at us on our own, friends and family would be only too eager to help if they thought someone was hurting the ones they love. Why don't we call on them for help earlier rather than later?

Maybe, just maybe life would have been better for me if I had admitted to my family and friends what was going on. I'm certain that if my dad had known the severity of the abusive actions I was being subjected to, he would have stepped in and put a stop to it. I look back and wish I had told family and friends what was going on. My hope is that if you read this, and realise you are in an abusive relationship, you think hard about letting loved ones know exactly what is going on. It's nothing to be ashamed of and is most certainly not your fault. The bravest thing you can do is to find your voice and talk about your situation. We are all stronger than we think. Weakness is to keep quiet and let it carry on. I let the abuse carry on .... for far too long!

Manipulative behaviour

I am sure that many of you who read my story will ask yourselves why on earth I continued in this relationship for so long. I understand why anyone would wonder how these types of relationships last for years and sometimes devastatingly, end in fatal circumstances. The one similar trait about men that are abusive is the manipulative nature they have. With a simple sentence they are able to convince the women that love them they are sorry. They have a way about them, a certain charm that gives hope they will change their ways.

Throughout our relationship Steve consistently used certain behaviours that I now know to be manipulative. Of course, I'm writing about my experiences in an abusive relationship but I could in all honesty be telling the story of so many other abusive relationships. It isn't my story in particular that I wanted to write about. Of course not, I mean, who am I? Why would anyone want to read about me in particular? Although, believe me, writing this has been a very cathartic experience. It is more the things to look out for and recognise that I wanted to highlight. For both the abused and for those who think a loved one may be experiencing such a relationship. This is the reason I decided to put pen to paper. We probably all have an idea what manipulation looks like, however I would like to show you what it looks like as it unfolds. As I mentioned earlier there are traits of behaviour to look for. Excessive apologising along with large amounts of attention that is given to the abused after an abusive act. Guilt trips that make you feel like you don't love enough, put downs that make you feel unworthy and fearful. Manipulative behaviour involves anger too. The manipulator can appear to get angry at certain situations to scare you into conforming to how he thinks you should be. Just one incident can condition you to feel you must avoid upsetting him at all cost! These are all classic signs of manipulation. Denial from the abuser is another classic manipulative behaviour. It slowly makes you think you're going mad. Did that just happen? Did I do something to make that happen? Did I deserve that? These are all questions I asked myself daily. Another behaviour is for the abuser to shift the blame. On many occasions in my case, Steve would tell his mother that I had started the fights and arguments. He would do this in front of me and other members of his family and play the victim himself. His punch line was "Mum, you just don't know what she's like!" This obviously led his family to believe I was indeed the argumentative and abusive one in the relationship. Invariably Steve would initiate an argument which at times resulted in a physical fight. He would then tell his mother that I had hit him (yes, on occasions I did) but this was as a result of sheer provocation and frustration. On those occasions he would fall to the floor as if I had knocked him out and lay there motionless. He made me feel as though I had really hurt him. It was this that would be aired to make his family feel sorry for him and not me. He would also use manipulative words and the knowledge that I loved him as a way back into the marital home. He always knew what buttons to press with me and I am sure this is true of other manipulators.

I hope these signs of manipulative behaviour give you more understanding of the story you are about to read. Often we don't realise when we have been manipulated and abused. It can sometimes be years after when realisation strikes. We encounter so many different personalities as we saunter through life. Some nice and some not so nice. To have a heads up on the not so nice personalities alongside physical and verbal abuse can only be a good thing, right? This is my story, I hope you gain an understanding and knowledge from it. After all knowledge is power....

JUST ME... THEN THERE WERE THREE

One...

I don't think of myself as a victim or a martyr and, oddly enough, after all I went through, I feel very strongly that what I endured was for a reason. As yet I'm not sure of the reason but I'm sure life will reveal it in a spectacular form. At this point in my life, if I was reading these experiences written by someone else I would be thinking, "Get a grip and finish this abusive relationship. Tell him to get out!" Believe me, I wanted to do that. Unfortunately at that point in my life I was very vulnerable and although I didn't realise it at the time I was also very depressed.

A few years before I had met Steve, I lost my mum to cancer. Anyone that has had to watch a loved one die of cancer will understand the effect it has on the family members having to watch it all happen. I was seventeen when mum died but fifteen when I was told about her illness. Throughout those two years I had to endure watching my beautiful, happy, loving mum wither into a skeletal shell of her former self. All the while I lived in denial of what the outcome of this disease would be even up until the last remaining days of her life. My parents kept the devastating consequences of cancer away from me, my sister and my brother. They never really spoke to us about what was more than likely to happen. So we lived in hope up until the end. Not the best way to manage a situation like that but they felt they were doing the right thing at the time. The final outcome (my mum's death) completely devastated us as a family and because of this we all seemed to drift away from each other. Each one of us left to cope with our feelings on our own. Me! Well I didn't really cope very well at all.

In the time between losing my mum and meeting Steve I went on regular drinking binges, never formed any lasting relationships with men so never knew what it was like for a man to treat me with love and respect. I thought one night stands and short flings were quite normal. I had however found myself a fantastic job and was on the road to a glittering sales career.

When I met Steve I was a naive twenty-two year old woman who was starting to think that maybe I should be in a long term relationship by now. Most of my friends were and I was starting to look for someone that I could hold onto for longer than a few weekends. The problem was I happened to meet a man that saw the potential not in me, but in the material things I had. I had a great job, I had my own home and a dad that lived in an affluent part of Cardiff. The man I met on the other hand had a job that didn't pay very well, no prospects and lived partly with his parents and partly in a council flat with the woman he had a child with when he was seventeen. When we met and started seeing each other on a regular basis he realised I had all these things and soon started to spend all his spare time at my house. He made me feel like I was the most special woman he had ever met. I met him whilst on a night out with my then sister in law. He squeezed past me whilst I was waiting to be served at a crowded bar. I was instantly attracted to him. He had dark blonde hair and a slight tan and his eyes were bright blue. He had a cast on his arm which created an avenue to an instant conversation. After our brief encounter he wandered back to his friends who were dancing madly on the small dance floor in the corner. His eyes constantly searched me out and when they found me they seemed to sparkle along with his cute smile. It wasn't long before we were deep in conversation and talking about meeting up.

The first couple of weeks into our relationship were fantastic and I thought I had finally met the man I was to spend the rest of my life with. When I think back there were times at the start of our relationship when he said some strange things but I just dismissed any throw-away remarks he made.

The problem with men like this is they manipulate you without you realising what is happening. At first each hurtful, nasty remark or demeaning action is said or done without you realising the meaning behind it. These things slowly eat away at your confidence and then all of a sudden you find you've lost years from your young life. I don't know if this type of man is clever or whether he doesn't realise at first what effect he's having on his partner, but what I do know is this manipulative type of behaviour makes childish boys feel like men.

So there I was a young woman finding my way after encountering a huge loss in my life but finding my way none the less. Then suddenly finding myself in a relationship I couldn't escape from. Two children followed and in what seems like no time at all there were three people in my life. I love my children and wouldn't wish that I was without them but Steve I could definitely live without. Unfortunately because I was scared of being a failure, I didn't want to admit to my dad or friends what was happening in my relationship and if only I had been brave enough to 'open up' to the people I loved then, it would have stopped the nightmare continuing week after week, month after month, year after year....

HOLIDAY ROMANCE

Two...

The week after I had struck up a relationship with Steve, he announced that he had booked a holiday with his mates just a few weeks before. I had no problem with that, after all we had only just met. Who was I to start telling him what he could or couldn't do? It was so early in our relationship and I really didn't want to be seen as 'that clingy girlfriend' so I told him I was fine with it. I didn't really want him to go but I felt I could trust him as our relationship was new and exciting.

The day he was to fly to Spain arrived and I woke with a sinking feeling in the pit of my stomach. We spent the morning together then I drove him to the airport. I can't remember exactly what was said on the way but I was a bit teary and Steve told me that he didn't really want to go. He said he would rather stay with me. By the time the holiday had arrived we had been going out for about five weeks, I had not met any of his friends he was going away with. We generally went out for drinks or had meals out on our own. Friends were never a part of what we did right from the start. At the time I didn't think much of it but looking back and having now experienced a 'normal' relationship I do find it a bit odd.

Anyway, I waved him off into the departure lounge where his friends were already waiting for him and drove back home. I wasn't looking forward to what seemed at the time a very long week ahead of me before he flew back home again. I was already missing him..

Whilst he was away he had asked me to drop a key to his parents' house. I had never met them before and again looking back, meeting my boyfriends family on my own without that said boyfriend is frankly a bit weird. I decided to drop the key that day as it was Saturday and it would give me something to do and I thought it would be nice to meet his mum and dad. When I got there I found all his family there; two sisters and partners with their brood, his brother and his baby too. I felt so uncomfortable. I was invited into the front room where everyone was assembled. I was most definitely the highlight of their day. I stayed for a short while but I couldn't wait to get out of there. Question after question was fired at me. It felt like no one knew he had met me and this was the first time they became aware of Steve having a girlfriend.

The week went by so slowly and how I missed him. He rang me and I felt he was missing me too. Although I felt excited every time he rang me, the phone would ring at inappropriate times. The shrill of the telephone in the middle of the night 1.00am, 2.00am, was there an emergency, was my dad ill? Questions that fly through your mind when the phone rings at that time in the morning. It was Steve. I think it was his way of checking up on me.

The week dragged by and at last, Saturday arrived! I set off to pick him up from the airport. I remember seeing the plane come in to land and the feeling of excitement was overwhelming. I made my way to arrivals and soon, there he was. He looked blonde, tanned and extremely handsome. We made our way home after Steve said a brief goodbye to his friends. I was looking forward to his company and getting back to having him around again. He didn't talk about his holiday much he just seemed to forget about it. Even when I asked him questions he snubbed them and didn't really give me any answers. A week or so later I saw a few photographs of him and his mates sitting around different bars with drinks in their hands; the usual photo's you would expect to see. I suppose if I'm honest I was looking at them to see if there were any girls in the pictures. There wasn't and I was happy. We put the holiday behind us and moved on.

A week or so went by and the holiday was not mentioned again. Then one Saturday morning I was pottering around the kitchen and looking for something in the drawers. Steve was upstairs getting ready to go to his football match as he did every Saturday morning. Suddenly there it was, staring up at me from the kitchen drawer as though it had been placed there for me to see. A photograph that made the blood drain from my face.

Steve and a dark haired girl sitting together in a deep embrace. Yes, kissing! Not on the cheek either! No, a french kiss. One of his friends had kindly captured the moment on camera. Who knows what else happened off camera! Ahhh! I couldn't believe it. I snatched the picture out of the drawer and flew upstairs screaming at him as I went. I thrust the picture in his face demanding an explanation. He couldn't say much really the evidence was there. He stammered and stuttered his way through his explanation. He well and truly wormed his way out of it really. He said it was a dare, a game they were playing. It wasn't what I thought, he kept saying. He very quickly grabbed his keys and wallet and disappeared through the door to get to his football match, promising he would be home early so that we could talk about it and sort it out.

He didn't come home that night or most of the next day. I wept for most of that weekend, the thought of him with another woman broke my heart, but I hoped we could sort it out. Little did I know this was to be the beginning of eight years of torment and ever so small and some not so small abusive acts from the man that claimed to have fallen in love with me....

NO FRIENDS ALLOWED

Three...

I remember a time early in my relationship with Steve when his bullying started to stop me interacting with my friends. This was a time before mobile phones-OMG! Can you imagine that? When friends wanted to talk they rang each other on land lines. I have to say this was something me and my friends did most nights and we would talk for hours. We talked about trivial things but never the less these trivial conversations were what bonded our friendships. I hadn't long moved into my first house and was enjoying my freedom and the grown up feeling of living on my own. It was only a few months after buying my house that I met Steve. Like any new couple in love we enjoyed the times we spent together and of course I dedicated myself and spent quality time with him. The nights he didn't stay were my nights to catch up with friends and gossip the evening away.

It wasn't long before Steve, yes Steve decided to move in with me full time. He made the suggestion. He thought it was silly for him to live at his parents when we could live together. Part of me was excited but there had been incidents with Steve that upset me and inside I was wondering if I should really let him move in with me. For example, at that time I had two kittens. I bought them when I moved into the house for company and I loved them dearly. On one occasion he kicked one of my kittens down the stairs because it was in his way. Surprised and annoyed I told him what I thought of him but he just laughed at me and carried on as if nothing unusual had happened. I did at the time wonder what else he was capable of if he could do that to a tiny creature. There was a part of me that was a little scared of him and I didn't want to upset him, so I said yes to him moving in. He subsequently moved all his clothes into my wardrobe. It wasn't long after I realised my friends were not phoning me as often as they usually did. More to the point I was not phoning them at all. I don't think I could tell you how or when it started but one night definitely sticks out in my mind more than others. Suddenly I realised why.

It was early evening and Steve and I were sitting watching television after having something to eat. My house was only a modest two-up-two-down so there was nowhere to escape to when one of us was on the phone. The phone rang and it was a friend of mine. I hadn't spoken to her for a while so I was really pleased to hear from her. We started chatting about nothing in particular but I do remember thinking I must not mention any men's names. Even then I must have subconsciously realised that was a trigger for him to start getting angry.

I had not been on the phone very long when all of a sudden a cushion flew at me. It hit me squarely in the face and took me quite by surprise. I dropped the phone and I remember missing some of what my friend was saying. It took a couple of seconds before I picked it up again and tried to compose myself. I was embarrassed to tell Victoria what had just happened and I just continued to listen. The whole time I was looking at Steve with a puzzled look on my face. I didn't know what I had said to make him do that but was aware I must have said something he didn't like. I carried on the conversation then whack! There was another cushion. This time it missed me and knocked over one of the ornaments on the window sill. I looked at Steve in astonishment. He was mouthing the words "Get of the **!*!! phone" I'll leave the expletive to your imagination. He repeated it over and over. Each time his voice was getting louder. He kept throwing objects at me and as I didn't want Vic to realise what was going on I made my excuses to get off the phone and said I would speak with her tomorrow.

Steve wouldn't explain to me what had made him do that, he just carried on watching television. He had a way of defusing an argument just by remaining silent. He could turn from being angry to looking like an angel within seconds. I remember sitting in silence until bedtime that evening, feeling slightly uncomfortable in his presence. After all I had done nothing wrong and yet he had made me feel like I was the most wicked person in the world.

I didn't realise it at the time but little by little he was manipulating me to conform to how he wanted me to be. I was becoming unsociable, scared to arrange nights out with friends in case he got angry with me. His nights out never stopped. In fact his nights out eventually led to weekends out. The point is, I was starting to become a shell of my former self. I could feel myself becoming quite introverted and I didn't know how to stop the downward spiral....

STAB NIGHT

Four...

It was a normal working day. We woke as usual, got up and got ready for work. There seemed nothing unusual about Steve that morning. He left for work early. I left the house shortly after him. I worked as a sales rep selling stationery. Steve didn't like me working as a rep. I think it was because he never really knew where I was, he couldn't keep track of me. His jealousy reared its ugly head frequently, even what I wore to work was scrutinised by him. He often remarked how I looked like a tart. I have to say though there wasn't then and isn't now anything over the top about how I look. Someone once told me I was quietly stunning. I'll take that! I've always perceived myself as being smartly dressed.

Steve worked for the local council at the time. I'm not really sure what he did. I know that sounds odd but that's how it was. Steve never did elaborate on his day to day duties. I think it was more to do with him not doing that much. He opened local toilet blocks and parks in the area first thing in the morning and his account of the day was always vague.

As I was saying. I left for work like any other normal working day. Mobile phones were not yet part of daily life for people so when we said goodbye in the morning it wasn't until we got home that we had a chance to speak to each other. My day was like any other working day really. A catch up over coffee in the office with my work friends in the morning, out on the road for most of the day visiting customers then back to the office around four o'clock to process any orders I had picked up in the day. At five o'clock I left for home knowing Steve was there waiting for me. If I was late, well let's just say my evening was not worth having. It was not always like that. Before I met Steve the office girls would more often than not wander over to the pub on the estate we worked on for a well deserved glass of wine before we all dispersed home. The day I'm remembering so vividly for you however was about to be anything less than normal.

Steve wasn't at home when I got back from work, which was slightly unusual but I didn't really think too much of it. It must have been seven o'clock when he finally walked through the door and when he did he was not in a very good mood. He wouldn't speak to me at all and whatever he did was followed by a look that could have killed. I started to feel scared and kept asking him if anything was wrong. I didn't get a reply though. As the atmosphere was so thick I decided to go up for a bath just to get away from his company. While I was in the bath I tried to think about what I may have done to annoy him. I was sure I hadn't done anything. I had not been out with friends and I was always at home when I should have been.

When I came back downstairs Steve seemed to have become more annoyed. His face was quite white and looked like thunder. That was it! I could not understand what was wrong. I asked him sternly what his problem was. I wished I had stayed quiet. It was as though something snapped in his head at the moment I asked him that question. He stormed into the kitchen and emerged with one of the kitchen knives. I shot out of my seat petrified. "What on earth are you doing?" I shouted. He was waving it at me screaming at the top of his voice. "Have you had any other boyfriends here?" "No!" I shouted back in amazement. "Not now" he screamed, before you met me, did you sleep here with anyone?" I couldn't believe what I was hearing. I was twenty three. Did he expect that I hadn't had any boyfriends before him? He had a little girl from a past relationship that I had embraced as part of my life. His ex was still very much part of our lives, (not in a good way) however it was something I was prepared to live with. We hadn't had 'that' conversation. You know the one where you're allowed to confess how many past partners you have had but I thought he would have realised I'd had relationships too. In his anger he seemed to just ignore what I was saying and started to come forward at me. I ran as fast as I could up the stairs and tried to lock myself in my bedroom by pushing

29

myself up against the door. I wasn't strong enough to keep him out of the room though and he was able to push the door open with ease. He flew into the room, still waving the kitchen knife around and screaming disgusting names at me left, right and centre. I was distraught and terrified. In tears I cowered in the corner of my tiny bedroom watching Steve as he started slashing my bed to shreds with the knife. He was like a man possessed. I had never seen him so angry. With such hatred he stabbed and dragged the knife across our bed until he had completely tired himself out. My mattress and sheets were shredded. When he finally stopped he ran downstairs and out of the front door. I could not move but was shaking and stayed curled in a ball for what seemed like hours. What I had just witnessed absolutely shocked me.

Eventually I managed to make my way down stairs to double lock the front door. I did not see Steve again that night and I was relieved at that, however I knew I would have to face him at some point the next day. I slept in the spare bedroom that night. I had set it up for when his daughter came to sleep over with us and it made me feel safe in there. If I closed my eyes and thought really hard I could imagine I was a girl again lying on my bed in the house I grew up in. Reality hit when I opened my eyes again though.

Not for one single moment did I think that was the last of my nightmare. Oh no! Somehow I knew there was plenty more to come and I was starting to think there was no way out of this existence for me. The problem was, I was terrified of him....

MY GLASGOW KISS

Five...

I remember receiving a wedding invitation from friends of mine I hadn't seen for a long time. I was over the moon that Vicky and Mike had thought to invite me, considering the length of time that had passed since I had seen either of them. My social life had dramatically disappeared since being with Steve due to him not liking any of my friends and not wanting me to socialise with them. I had grown up through high school with Vic and I had known Mike since my early teenage years so I considered them close friends. I needed to broach the subject of us going to the wedding carefully and choose my time but I had decided in my mind that we were definitely going, I was determined to be there.

When I finally mentioned it to Steve, he had an excuse not to go, which of course I was expecting. He had been invited out for a friend's birthday. Yes, Steve alone had been invited. I was never invited to anything that went on in his social world. Anyway I put my foot down and insisted that we were going to Vicky and Mike's wedding. I argued the length of time that had passed since I had seen them. I remember getting a bit emotional with my argument and I think the tears won the day. Or so I thought! (Little did I know he had other plans for the day that did not manifest until the day of the wedding...). That aside I was so excited. I started thinking about what to wear. Money was extremely tight but I wanted to look great. It's funny I worked full time and Steve was living with me but I didn't ever see any money from him to help with my mortgage and bills. On top of that, he would help himself to my bank card and take whatever he needed to ensure his weekends were full of drink and fun. I just didn't realise the scale of what he was spending at the time.

The wedding day arrived and I had scrimped and saved money to buy the happy couple a wedding present. I remember not being able to afford to buy sellotape so had to stick the paper down with buff packaging tape from the warehouse where I worked. (Oh my goodness, when I think about that now it just makes me laugh.) Anyway we set of for the wedding that day with me as the designated driver. As usual Steve was the one that was drinking that day. I only agreed to this to keep the peace. If I hadn't I don't think he would have gone so I played subservient yet again. The church service was beautiful. I was sitting next to a friend I hadn't seen for a long time and we laughed and joked and just thoroughly enjoyed each others company throughout the service. Steve looked so out of place and not at all happy. It didn't help that my friend was a guy but I just didn't care. When I look back at how I was in the church that day it tells me the fun loving, young girl I was still existed deep inside but it felt like Steve made sure that girl was locked in a dark cupboard so no one saw her. I just didn't know why he wanted to do that.

Next we were off to the reception at the Celtic Manor Hotel. This is where my day started going wrong. Steve as I mentioned earlier had other ideas about how the day would pan out. He insisted that as soon as we had eaten the reception meal that we drive back into Cardiff to have a birthday drink with his friend. I couldn't believe it. However knowing Steve I didn't dare refuse. I agreed as long as it was one drink and then back to my friends wedding. He said yes but of course that didn't happen. Whilst at the pub with his friends I was left on my own while he disappeared off somewhere and I didn't see him for quite a while. The moment he re-appeared I insisted we leave and go back to the hotel. I was so upset at being left on my own at a pub I didn't know with people I didn't know and on top of that having to leave my friend's wedding half way through.

Finally we arrived back at the hotel and I immediately made a bee-line for my friends and the secure feeling of being with people I liked. Steve went silent and stayed that way for the rest of the evening. I tried to involve him in conversations but to no avail. There was one particular conversation I had however that killed the evening completely. I introduced Steve to an old friend. It was a guy I had dated but Steve didn't know this and nothing in our conversation even suggested we had dated but Steve took an instant dislike to him. His name was Jock and he was introducing me to his new wife. I hadn't been speaking with them for long before Steve started behaving even more oddly than he had all day. He pulled me away from the couple and announced that we were going home. I wanted to refuse but at that point in the evening I didn't dare. Steve was very drunk and not a nice drunk at that. I barely said any goodbyes because I was frog marched out into the car park. There as we stood next to our car I was pushed to the floor. Steve stood over me yelling disgusting names at me. He accused me of talking to an old boyfriend and he wanted to know if we had slept together. I denied it because we hadn't but he would not listen to anything I said back to him.

Once again I was terrified of his over-bearing presence. He wasn't a tall man, in fact probably 5ft 3" in bare feet but boy, his temper made him seem huge. I gathered myself up off the floor and tried to get into the car. Steve grabbed the keys out of my hand and head butted me with force (I didn't see that one coming). I stumbled and fell to the ground again. Shocked and slightly concussed, I was pulled up and flung into the passenger side of the car. In a drunken rage, he jumped into the driver's side and started to drive at speed out of the car park. There was a single track lane that led back to the motorway and he drove dangerously fast down this narrow lane. I was screaming at the top of my voice for him to stop but my words were ignored. I was holding onto whatever I could to stop myself from being thrown through the windscreen if we crashed. I had a vision of a car coming the other way and everyone involved being killed outright. It was sheer luck that nothing had come the other way that night. My tears and screams were blood curdling throughout the fast journey home. Steve drove the few junctions down the motorway at horrendous speed too. I had made my mind up to run off as soon as we arrived back home. That is exactly what I did. He pulled up on the drive outside the house and I flung open the car door and ran as fast as I could to the main road. I flagged down the first taxi I saw and made my way to my sister's house the other side of Cardiff. I was so relieved to have escaped him. In tears, bruised and shaking with fear, I knocked on her front door. She opened the door and with a look of shock and concern on her face she bundled me in. I was safe but I knew it was not for long....

LITTLE BY LITTLE

Six...

Although there were countless occasions of abuse I can
share with you a huge amount of the abuse I withstood
was so slight, it was such a small almost insignificant
moment I didn't really think of it as abuse at the time. It
is only when I look back and remember certain things
he did or said that made me feel worthless that I realise
it all added to the bigger picture. Everything he did was
designed to undermine me. I want to share the smaller
acts of abuse with you as well as the enormously big
events that happened in our relationship.

After work one day we decided to go and buy a new
television. I was still in my work clothes and was
wearing a skirt and blouse that day. It was something I
wore to work regularly and also something I felt
comfortable wearing. At the shop we browsed for a bit
until we had chosen the television we wanted. We called
the salesman over and started the process of the sale.
The salesman took us to a booth and as I was paying
(surprise surprise) I sat next to the salesman to give my
card details and house number for delivery. You know
how it goes! Steve sat next to me and throughout the

sale he glanced at me from time to time. As I was concentrating on what the salesman was saying I ignored Steve's looks and continued our conversation. Purchase over, delivery date set, we walked out of the shop. The moment we left the shop Steve leaned in close to me and whispered "Your a**!*! ing slut!" He took me by surprise and I wanted to know why and what he meant. Well it turned out that Steve had thought my skirt was too short and he suggested I wore it to be provocative. Throughout the sale I had not noticed the salesman be anything other than professional and I didn't feel uncomfortable talking to him at all. Anyway, Steve was sitting right next to me! However Steve managed to make me feel like a slut for wearing a skirt that sat slightly higher than my knees when I sat down. It only took one nasty comment from him to scare me and the thought of him thinking I looked like a slut was powerful enough for me to stop wearing that skirt again.

Another time, Steve took a dislike to the shorts I used to wear around the house. They were an old pair of jeans that I had cut above the knee. They were comfortable and I liked the look of them on me. We were sitting watching television when he turned to face me quite suddenly. He grabbed my leg then grabbed hold of the shorts and tore them from the knee to the crutch. His only excuse for doing this was that he didn't like them on me. For peace sake I decided to throw them away and forget the incident but could not understand why he had done that.

A lot of the abuse was name calling and when I say name calling I mean the most disgusting things you can think of. I think it was just his way of reminding me he was in charge and making me feel worthless.

Another vile thing he used to do was spit in my face. The first time he did it I felt physically sick. We were having an argument about him going out every weekend. I think because he knew I was right about us not having the money for him to drink away every weekend, and not having a retaliation argument he just spat instead. The feeling of his saliva on my face was putrid.

Steve was always putting me down in ways that would make me feel like I wasn't good enough. This went on throughout the years in our relationship. The things he did and the things he said had a slow but steady downward spiraling effect on me and eventually I believed the things he said about me were true. He also turned every argument around and blame me for starting them. I often questioned myself and started to think all the arguments were indeed my fault. My confidence throughout diminished month by month, year by year. I couldn't buy new clothes or make up I just made do with what I had. I rarely went out with friends and when I did, there was a beating waiting for me when I got home. So slowly but surely I stopped going out. I didn't live I just survived....

LOVE BITES

Seven...

When I think of love bites they make me think of sex and passion. They tend to be given in the throws of a passionate embrace or encounter. Right!? The result isn't pretty, well I don't think so, however if I notice a hickey on someone I tend to think "Oooh naughty!" Ha-ha. I'm not doing a very eloquent job of trying to say that although unsightly they are usually a product that has stemmed from a nice experience.

Well, Steve went through a faze of giving me love bites. (Not on my neck where you would expect to see them.) No! On my face! They were not given to me in a passionate embrace either. Steve would grab hold of me when I was least expecting it and pin me to the settee or the floor and suck different parts of my face. He would pretend he was just play fighting and leave little red marks on my face knowing I would not be able to hide them. There was method behind his madness. I mentioned in an earlier story that he hated me doing the job that I did. I was out all day visiting customers and when I wasn't out with customers I was in the office with my work friends. It was the thought of me

45

interacting with other men that was too much for him to bear. He hated the thought of any other man thinking I was attractive. The first time he sucked my face I laughed it off even though I was so angry at what he had done. In the morning I covered the bites with concealer the best I could before I set off for work. If they were noticeable nobody mentioned anything to me. The second time there were more to cover and they were darker, more intense, more noticeable. Again nobody mentioned anything but I knew they were visible. I felt so embarrassed. Can you imagine having to go to work with love bites on your face? Steve was determined to ruin my career. I don't know why as I brought home a good wage. If I wasn't working how would we manage financially? I think the thoughts he had of me while I was at work were too debilitating for him. He could not think of the big picture and I'm certain he never thought further than what he was going to do each weekend.

I was the one that suffered for this in the most humiliating and horrible ways. My boss was already starting to notice my tardiness and my appearance and standards of dress were definitely not what they used to be. Not only due to lack of money for new clothes but I was so unsure of what I should wear too. It was safe to say my confidence had gone. I needed help. I needed my family and friends. No one was there anymore. I suddenly realised I was going through this alone. I was still putting on a brave face, a facade that everything was okay. In reality I was living a nightmare existence, how could I dig my way out of this dark abyss ....

THE UNFORTUNATE PROPOSAL

Eight...

The evening Steve proposed to me wasn't exactly the romantic experience I had dreamt of as a little girl. It turned out to be the end result of a night out that turned sour.

The friends I had at this point in my life were all work mates. I had struck up a close friendship with Jan a lady I worked with. She was older than me and I think she took me under her wing and could see how much I had changed over the short time I had been with Steve. Jan was getting married and had invited us both to the wedding party in the evening. Everyone from work would be there too. On the night of the party Steve and I decided to drive as getting a taxi would prove too expensive. We could not afford to stay over night anywhere so I agreed to drive so Steve could have a drink. It was always me that drove when we were out with people that I knew. Steve was so awkward in the company of strangers that I always thought if he had a drink he would relax and let me enjoy my friends' company. It never worked out like that though.

We eventually reached the party after getting slightly lost on the way. We arrived to find all my work mates and their partners there and the party was in full swing. Steve had met most of the people I worked with a few times so I hoped he would be more relaxed than usual on this occasion. After we had said our congratulations to Jan and her new husband we made our way to the bar. Frazer (another rep at the company I worked for) was at the bar ordering a round of drinks. As soon as he saw me he gave me a big hug and insisted on buying our drinks too. He shook Steve's hand and as they had met before, I felt comfortable leaving Steve to help Frazer. They brought the drinks over to the group from the office that had gathered around a huge table situated close to the dance floor. I felt so happy that night. I was having fun and hadn't felt so relaxed on a night out for some time. I thought Steve was enjoying himself too. He was chatting to a few of the work lads that drove the delivery vans for the company and as Steve had just successfully secured himself a new job as a delivery driver I was sure they would get on well. I felt relaxed and I dropped my guard completely that night. Stupidly I was thinking we were a happy, normal couple enjoying a night out with friends. Frazer asked me to get up and dance and in my relaxed state I agreed. His wife was goading me on to dance. I knew her very well and I knew she didn't mind.

Steve on the other hand did mind, unaware of his feelings I just continued to have fun. When Steve noticed me enjoying (might I say) a ridiculous dance with Frazer he started to make his way to the dance floor. He didn't really do anything that anyone except me would have noticed. It was more the look he gave me when he joined us dancing. I knew straight away he was not happy with me and it was at that moment that I remembered just who I had come out with. I made my excuses to Frazer, you know the gestures! The ones where you flap your hands in front of your face to suggest your hot and then the tipping of the hand up to your mouth to suggest you need a drink. I laughed and walked off the dance floor. It wasn't long before Steve joined me at the table. His face was like thunder. "We're going" he said quite forcefully! I just accepted that fact and dragged my coat off the back of one of the chairs. I managed to say goodbye to few friends made a few excuses and walked out of the social club. Once in the car park I knew I was in for it.

In a rage Steve decided that he would drive home as he had on other occasions. I silently sat myself in the passenger side and waited terrified at what was to come. Steve remained quiet until we were driving at speed down the motorway. That was when the angry accusations started. Supposedly I was having an affair with Frazer and had apparently had relationships with the majority of the guys I worked with. I was in tears. My denials once again fell on deaf ears and I withstood verbal abuse that would make your grandmother's toes curl the whole journey home. In the midst of this verbal abuse he was trying to feel my body. His left hand groped wherever it could. I was pushing him off screaming for him to leave me alone but this made him more and more angry. I felt sick at his touch.

We finally arrived home. I ran into the house and sat on the settee with my head in my hands completely broken. Steve walked in quietly and sat next to me. His angry manner had disappeared. He was quite calm. I sat back nervously I didn't know what to expect next. He lay on his back and put his head in my lap. He lay there silently for what seemed like an eternity. Then quite suddenly he turned his head and looked at me. "Will you marry me?" he asked. I looked at him with tears in my eyes. Tears of fear not joy! I could not say no I was certain I would get a beating if I did. So after a few moments and in a very quiet voice I said yes. Not meaning it but just wanting that evening to end. In my mind I thought he would forget all about the proposal in the morning. Of course I was wrong....

MY SPARKLER

Nine...

OK! I said yes to marrying someone I was not happy with. Someone who brought me down at every turn, someone who wasn't the full picnic! However the fact was I did say yes...

The problem with being in an abusive relationship is feeling that you can't admit what is going on. It's a feeling of failure. I didn't want my family or my friends to know exactly what was happening to me. I wanted them to think I was in a happy, loving relationship. I felt that if I told anyone what was going on they would think badly of me in some way and that I was a complete failure in my life. Which ironically I was! So, I would make excuse after excuse for him. Excuses for his behaviour, excuses as to why bruises had appeared on me and this time it was an excuse as to why my future husband had not yet bought me an engagement ring. The one thing a girl wants to show the world her man loves her is a beautiful engagement ring right? Honestly, I personally don't think it's what ring you get given, it's just actually receiving a ring. Whatever size, shape or stone. It's just the gesture! Well I didn't have one. Steve had not produced a ring the night of his proposal. He obviously didn't think the whole proposal thing through! It was a very spur of the moment thing but I thought a ring would probably follow. Weeks went by. **Nothing!** I dropped hints every now and then because of course I wanted to show my friends the gesture of love my boyfriend had given me. As yet with no sign of a ring, I started thinking of ways to suggest we postpone the wedding. We didn't have any money saved and I had no idea how we were going to pay for it. I wasn't sure how Steve would react to such a suggestion but considering he hadn't bought a ring I was hoping that maybe he would be glad of the suggestion. So one day as we were driving to do a food shop I brought the subject up. I took the line of waiting and saving money so we didn't get ourselves in debt thinking this was quite a logical argument. Oh! I wish I had stayed quiet. Steve immediately started accusing me of not loving him, and spouted out how he would marry me tomorrow if he could. Why was it I wanted to wait? His angry accusations once again caused me to feel like the bad guy. That shopping trip was strained after that, once again I felt anxious and frightened.

After months had gone by I decided I needed to take charge so I insisted we meet in town after work one evening and take a look around some jewellers. It was almost as though the ring would make everything right. It was a symbol to me that everything going on in the relationship might stop. The day arrived when we were to meet and choose my ring. I was excited and of course had told everyone in work I was getting my engagement ring later that day. Everyone was expecting to see it the following morning. That evening we wondered around the shops glancing into jewellers shop windows. My eyes were wide with amazement at the glitter and glamour of the rings in the windows. The lights shone on the diamonds and they glistened, screaming at me to try them on. I don't think Steve even looked, he showed no interest. He stood slightly behind me in a bit of a daze, probably wondering what on earth he had done. I didn't care. I was having one of those rings. Eventually we wandered into one of the shops and sat down to try on a ring I liked. It was beautiful! I tried it on and it fitted my finger perfectly. This was the one I wanted. It said MY MAN LOVES ME! Ha-ha you gotta laugh. The lady took Steve's card details and I beamed with joy. After a few minutes the lady looked up with a sympathetic look on her face. "I'm afraid the bank won't allow the payment" she said. "Do you have any other form of payment?" "No!" was Steve's answer. We apologised profusely and made a sharp exit from the shop. I was mortified. Steve had no money, of course he couldn't buy me a ring. What the hell was I going to do? I was not going home without an engagement ring so I insisted we keep looking. Eventually we wandered into a smaller jewellers and I noticed quite a cute ring. It had three heart shapes. Two small hearts on each side of a slightly larger heart. The hearts had slithers of diamonds placed in each of them. It was understated but it was pretty. There was definitely something I liked about it. It was not very expensive and so I told Steve I would buy it on my card if he gave me the money back. He agreed. When I look back I realise he had no intention of buying me a ring. He knew he didn't have the money for that. Of course I knew deep down too. I didn't really think I would see the money but I had to justify buying my own engagement ring.

Well, that was that! I had bought my own engagement ring. Not quite the sparkler I had in mind. Yet again I had feeling of failure. Nobody ever knew. I showed off my ring the next day in work and hid the truth behind a false smile....

MY HEN....DON'T

Ten

I remember the night of my hen do very well as I'm sure any married woman does. My memories are not fond memories unfortunately, I think I blocked out some of the good ones.

It was Saturday night two weeks before my wedding and a small group of us decided to go to see a tribute band. I honestly can't remember who they were a tribute too, I think what happened paled into insignificance when I got home. I think I mustered up five friends altogether for my hen night. I was determined to have a good time and enjoy my hen do as I hadn't had a night out for quite a while. The tribute band were performing at a venue outside of Cardiff. The venue was a bit too far away to get a taxi and as Steve had refused to take us my friend's husband agreed to take us and pick us up whenever we were ready. I know a tribute band in a quiet venue far from clubs and pubs in the middle of nowhere sounds a bit strange for a young hen but that was what I felt comfortable with. A night clubbing would have created arguments and accusations and I could not cope with that so I opted for a quieter option. That night we all eventually arrived at the venue and started what turned out to be a great evening. I do remember enjoying the band and dancing around the tables with my friends. It goes to show it really doesn't matter where you go on a night out as long as you have people you care about around you.

We danced, sang and drank. We even spoke with the band after the show. I had quite a bit to drink and I felt relaxed and carefree. I really didn't want the evening to end. That night Steve had said he was going out with his friends and so I thought he wouldn't be home until the following afternoon. (That was his usual habit). I had told Steve I wouldn't be back too late, probably around midnight. Time flew that evening and I didn't know what time it was when Vicky's husband picked us up. I didn't worry though because as I said I thought the house would be empty when I got home. We pulled up outside my house and I stumbled out of the car waving and shouting my goodbyes to the remaining girls that were being dropped home. I made my way to the front door and pushed the key into the lock. At that moment the door flew open! I remember falling through the door as it opened in shock. It was Steve, he had opened the door just at the moment I was about to push it open. He didn't help me up, he just went and sat back down on the settee where he had set up an alarm clock by his side. As I stumbled into the front room he stood up and thrust the clock in front of my face. **"It's two o'clock!"** He boomed. (It's funny how quickly you can sober up when fear takes hold). **"You said you'd be back by twelve!"** he boomed again. I didn't know what to say, I froze. "It's my hen night!" I eventually cried. That didn't matter to him, he was overcome with anger and jealousy. I have no idea what he thought I was doing. He knew exactly where I was going and who I was with. I was also in no doubt he had checked the venue to make sure what I said was going on was true.

What happened next was horrific and something nobody should have to go through.

I was dragged into the kitchen and thrown to the floor. Accusations flying at me all the while. I crawled into the corner of my small galley kitchen and cowered next to my fridge. There was nowhere to hide! Steve in a rage took a few paces towards me and started kicking me as hard as he could. I cowered curled up tight into a ball. It was my right thigh and side that took the brunt of the beating. Over and over and over again! After a while I couldn't feel the pain I just took it until it stopped. Stacked on the other side of the kitchen were a set of car tyres. Steve often had scrap to sell on. Once he had finished his attack he turned and as he walked passed the tyres he kicked them in anger. Oh my god! Talk about divine retribution.

He broke his toes! That stopped him in his tracks and

he hopped around screaming at the top of his voice. His anger disappeared and turned to tears instead. I didn't care, I crawled upstairs to the spare room and curled up in bed. Shaking, crying and petrified I lay there just waiting for the morning.

I don't know where he slept that night but in the morning he slid himself into bed next to me and cuddled in. It was his way of trying to be forgiven. After hurting me he would cuddle me and hope I would dismiss what had happened the night before. I froze! I lay in his unwanted tender grip in silence. Tears streaming down my face, I wished I was dead....

WEDDING DAY BLUES

Eleven...

I honestly thought long and hard about what I could tell you about my wedding day. The thing is there wasn't one thing in particular that stood out. There were lots of little things.

From the moment I opened my eyes on my wedding day I felt lonely. I spent the eve of my wedding at home on my own. Steve had spent that evening with his friends and was sleeping at his parents house and was leaving for the church from there. My wedding morning consisted of getting up, bathing, trying to curl my hair and generally feeling quite sick with fear. The wedding was at two o'clock and when you're waiting on your own time drags. My dad, sister and niece arrived at about twelve o'clock. Steve's daughter was dropped off at my house around about the same time. My niece and Steve's daughter were my bridesmaids and they looked like little princess's in their dresses. They all waited in the front room while I went upstairs to step into my wedding dress. My friend Jan from the office called at the house to check I was ok and my dad sent her up to my bedroom to see me. Just as I was stepping into my wedding dress she entered my bedroom. At once she noticed the bruises all the way down my right thigh. I felt so embarrassed. I remember making some excuse for them, however she didn't look as though she believed me. Anyway, Jan helped me button my dress at the back and arrange my flowing long veil then followed me downstairs to my waiting family. Shortly after that we left for the church. Jan and her husband drove me in their car. They had a posh looking Rover and they were happy to act as chauffeur for the day. My bridesmaids followed in my sister's boyfriend's car. It wouldn't have been the best looking wedding convoy you would have ever seen but it was cost effective! It was a budget wedding and as I had taken out a two thousand pound loan to pay for the day, I had to be as frugal as possible.

The wind was so strong that day, I remember trying to keep my veil from flying off my head as I stepped out of the car. I walked through the church graveyard whilst beckoning my young bridesmaids to hurry and tried desperately to stay looking bride like. We all came to a stop in the small church porch whilst waiting for the music to que my walk down the aisle. It was there the most poignant moment of the day happened for me. As I stood arm in arm with my dad he looked at me with tears in his eyes. Looking back at him with tears in my eyes I desperately wanted him to see how unhappy I was. Dad is a very clever man. A man of very few words and unfortunately back then I never felt comfortable talking to him about my problems. I always felt he was still grieving for my mum and never wanted to add to his worry. However I desperately wanted him to say "come on let's just go home" and whisk me back to the house I grew up in. That moment passed in an instant and the music started. My dad and I walked slowly down the aisle. I don't remember smiling once! I came to a stand still next to Steve then my dad passed my hand to him. I looked at Steve and he looked back at me. "I can still see your spot!" he said under his breath. Yes! honestly can you believe it? That always makes me laugh now. I mean what was I doing marrying this man? Too late, it was done, we'd exchanged vows. The ceremony was over and all of a sudden Steve and I were walking back down the aisle as man and wife.

The reception was at my dads house so the day before the wedding I had spent my time making the house look beautiful. Ribbons, bows, balloons, it really did look stunning. I started to feel a little excited. It was short lived though. (If you could have seen it the morning after the reception you would have thought I'd had a teenagers house party.) Steve's friends basically trashed my dad's home. There was urine all over the toilet floor, wine and beer trodden into the carpets, food in places food should not be and garden ornaments in my dad's fish pond. My dad's garden was his pride and joy, he had toiled in that garden for years making it a beautiful oasis and in seconds Steve's friends turned it into a children's playground. My brother in law inhaled the gas from the balloons over my wedding cake and spoke in a squeaky voice to anyone that would listen to him. Steve's mum decided it was her job to cut my wedding cake and sliced into it in front of my eyes. Oh and Steve disappeared to go and see his ex with his daughter. Honestly you couldn't make it up!

I felt so uncomfortable in the house I had so many happy memories and there at my own wedding reception it felt as though I was in a stranger's house. I remember walking around the house, wondering who most of the guests were. When Steve finally got back from visiting his ex I insisted we leave for the hotel room we had booked for that night. There we freshened up and made ourselves ready for the evening party.

This turned out to be as bad as the reception. I was truly glad when it was over. My family decided not to attend in the evening and only a handful of my friends came along. The rest of the guests were Steve's friends and family. That say's a lot doesn't it! We had laid on a buffet which when I think back looked dreadful. More children's party than wedding party. The evening continued in a similar vein. During the evening I was dragged across the dance floor by Steve in my wedding dress. He had tipped me over while dancing and I fell onto my bum so he thought it would be funny to drag me by my arm across the floor. My friends made a comment after wondering why he had done that?

There was a point in the evening when Steve and his friends lined up on the dance floor. I can't tell you who decided to do this but they all decided to take their trousers down. Steve attempted it until I intervened. At the end of the night as I was trying to find Steve so we could leave and make our way back to the hotel I caught him smoking drugs with one of his work friends. It was only about twelve o'clock but that was it! I couldn't take any more. In tears I stormed out onto the main road. Steve followed me out and ran after me down the road. As the guests carried on partying we walked down a busy main road arguing as we went. We attempted to flag down a taxi in between harsh words, me in a filthy wedding dress and him in his suit. We must have looked hilarious to people driving passed.

Finally we arrived back at the hotel room where the end of the night was less than passionate. After stepping out of my bedraggled dress I collapsed on the bed as did Steve and we both crashed out until the next morning.

That was my wedding day! From beginning to end it disappointed ......

SIGNS

Twelve...

Have you ever had the feeling that you shouldn't be doing something? There are signs as you wander along life's path, so big they almost shout **"DON'T DO THIS"** at you. They are almost deafening but you do it anyway. Then in hindsight after its all gone wrong you wish you had taken notice. Well, there were a few of these signs and, no, I didn't take any notice of them. Deep down I knew they were signs to stop me doing something but I carried on regardless.

One of those signs was losing my wedding dress. Just a few weeks before the wedding the shop I had bought my wedding dress from went into administration and all their stock was carted off to a warehouse in the welsh valleys. It took a couple of weeks to find out exactly where it had gone but eventually I found myself sifting through hundreds of dresses in a cold, dark and dusty storage unit. Finally I found it. I carefully gave it the once over to make sure there were no dirty marks or rips then gathered it up in my arms and took it home. Once home I took it straight to my bedroom and tried it on only to find it drowned me. The worry had taken it's toll and I had lost a lot of weight. I have to say I was not very big to begin with so the extra weight I had lost was starting to make me look quite drawn and unhealthy. However the dress had to be altered. Lost and altered from the original design. That sign was screaming at me.

Can I take you now to the night after my wedding day. We had spent the wedding night in a hotel but the next night we were back home. That evening whilst looking through our wedding gifts and cards we watched our wedding video. As a gift Frazer had filmed the day and overnight made sure we had it to watch the next day. We drank quite a few glasses of wine that evening. Actually when I think about it I drank far more than I would normally. The result of which put me in a deep sleep that night. That all sounds quite normal I suppose for a couple celebrating their marriage however the sign came loud and clear the next morning. I woke mid morning with a very cloudy head and made my way downstairs. BANG! There was the sign. We had been burgled. The front room window had been left wide open so had the front door. All our wedding presents were gone along with my handbag and video recorder. Yes the video of our wedding too. As you can imagine I was stunned, shocked and very upset. Steve flew downstairs after hearing my screams. After we had looked around and realised just how much had been taken we called the police and started the process that follows a burglary. When I think back to that morning the sign was yelling out loud and clear **'This wedding was not meant to have happened!'** My house was in a quiet street in a respectable area. I often wonder who really would have known those presents were in that particular house that night. I'll let you draw your own conclusions about how this burglary happened. To be honest I have my own theory!

If there is one of many things I have taken from my time in this bad relationship it is to take notice of certain events trying to guide me down paths I should or should not take. I can honestly say by doing that my life is all the better for it....

RAMPAGE

Thirteen...

There were countless evenings when Steve and I had huge arguments resulting from things Steve did. However, one stands out in my mind as though it were yesterday.

It was a weekend like many others in some ways. Steve had done his usual trick and left the house early Saturday morning to go to his football match with the line I had heard so many times before. "I'll be home early tonight love!" "I'm not feeling very well this morning anyway." (Oh lord if only I had a pound for every time he had said that.) Well as predicted he did not come home early he did his usual and it was Sunday evening when I saw him next. This time it was different than most Sunday evenings. The norm was he sauntered home just after mid day, sober and begging for my forgiveness. His mouth was usually flowing with excuse after excuse as to why he had stayed out all weekend again. Inevitably an argument would follow. This particular Sunday he did not arrive home until at least six o'clock. He banged on the front door quite unable to use his key. He was as drunk as a lord. In fact I had never seen him so drunk. I opened the front door not scared this time but angry. He couldn't speak and how he had managed to get home in that state I'll never know.

I was so fed up with his antics every weekend. You see by now we had a little boy. He was only a year old at the time and my weekends consisted of working Saturday mornings in a local supermarket because I had lost my sales job. To be honest I had lost my job because I had taken on the extra work on the weekends with the supermarket due to Steve being sacked from his job. We needed the extra money so I had to make up the short fall with extra work. After having my son I was back working at the stationery company after a month and also working weekends. Something had to give and as my image had slipped and my enthusiasm had too it was the full time job I couldn't hold onto. So, on this particular weekend after working, motherly duties to a young baby and household chores you can imagine I was not best pleased to see my husband in the state he was in after a wonderful weekend of partying. Anyway like I said I opened the door angry and wanting to know where he had been until this time and of course why he was so drunk. Wrong thing to do again! The moment I had shouted at him for answers his face turned to thunder. He immediately started to throw whatever he could get his hands on at me. Picture frames, telephone, flower vases, you name it he threw it! He started to overturn the furniture too. The settee was pushed over and the curtains torn off the rails. I was petrified once again. I was concerned for my little boy upstairs asleep in his cot. I froze. I cowered in the corner of the room while Steve rampaged through the house. He didn't stop in the front room he made his way to the kitchen. With one swoop of his arm he knocked everything on the work top off onto the floor including the microwave my brother had given us as a wedding present. The kitchen table was knocked over; and the immense roar he made whilst doing this was overwhelming.

Whilst he was in the kitchen I made a run for it upstairs. I grabbed Daniel from his cot, blankets and all. I ran downstairs and out of the front door. I didn't look behind me in case Steve wasn't far behind. I shouldn't have worried though he was not aware of what I had done at all. I ran to a neighbour who I had made friends with while working in the supermarket. In tears I knocked on her door as loud as I could. She ushered me and Dan in with a shocked look on her face. "What on earth is going on?" she said. She sat me down and tried to calm me whilst her husband made me a cup of tea. In tears I told her what had happened. She couldn't believe what she was hearing. She insisted I phone his parents. I didn't really want to but I knew deep down I could not sort this out on my own. I'm glad I did they were outside my house in a few minutes. I walked over to meet them, leaving Daniel with my friend.

I didn't have a key for the front door with me as I had left so abruptly. The door had slammed behind me and the back door was locked as well. Steve's dad took a look through the window of the back door. Through that window you could see through the kitchen into the front room and what he saw fired his temper in a split second. He took a run at the door and with his shoulder smashed the door open. As all three of us entered the upturned house what we witnessed was quite a sad sight really. Steve had passed out in the middle of the mangled front room. He had taken all his clothes off except his boxer shorts and was spread-eagled on his back. His blushes weren't spared either shall I say! Steve's dad lunged at at him. He dragged him up off the floor and shook him as hard as he could. Steve's mum was in tears. She was muttering through her tears that the marriage should end. Absolutely disgusted, his parents told me that Dan and I were to stay at their house that night and that they would help me clear up in the morning. I was in such a daze I agreed with them. By this time my friend had made her way over with Daniel. She gave me a hug and assured me everything would be alright.

His parents gave up their bed for me that night and with Daniel in a make shift cot next to me. I tried to sleep. I didn't sleep though. I don't remember crying that night. I think I was more in shock than anything else. I was dreading the next day I knew I would have to face Steve. My home had been destroyed and I did not want to see the mess in the cold light of day. I remembered Steve's mum saying she thought the marriage should end and I kept thinking about what I should do.

Was this the end of our marriage? I was hoping it was, I so wanted this nightmare to end....

PUSH; PUNCH; ANYTIME OF THE MONTH

Fourteen...

Domestic abuse comes in a full range of different guises and everything that an abused individual goes through is more often than not kept from friends and family. Usually because the abused individual feels they may have done something to deserve being treated so badly. They fear that what they tell people may not be believed or that they are making a mountain out of a molehill. So Steve managed to get away with incidents that made me wonder if he meant to do these particular things or if they had been accidents. Let me give you an example.

There was a period of time when I woke regularly in the early hours of the morning with a terrible pain in my back. The pain would wake me, then for a while I would feel quite disorientated. It was always in my lower back but it never felt like muscular pain. Oddly it always felt like I had been punched with great force. I knew there was only one person that could have done that. The person lying next to me! However when I looked at

Steve he always looked like he was sleeping soundly. I would just give my back a rub and try to settle and get back to sleep. This happened on countless occasions. The morning after I would wonder if it actually happened or if I had been dreaming. Then one night I happened to have trouble getting to sleep. I just lay in bed thinking, as you do. Suddenly BAM! There was the pain. I could not believe it. It was Steve. He had punched me full force at the bottom of my spine. It was agony. I turned to Steve with tears welling in my eyes. As usual he looked as though he was fast asleep but I knew what he had done. I had felt his body tense next to me as he swung his arm into my back. "What did you do that for?" I asked with a quiver in my voice. "What?" He said sleepily. "I know you punched me!" I said. Steve just denied it and told me to go back to sleep. I lay there yet again with tears streaming down my face. All this time it had been Steve. Whatever had I done to deserve that? I know now it wasn't anything I had done it was just his way of breaking me that little bit more.

On other occasions I was pushed into things for no reason. One Christmas he pushed me into the Christmas tree. He was pretending to mess around with me. You know gentle pushing and winding me up about something. I forget what now. The point being his excuse for what happened next was that he was only playing. I was standing next to the Christmas tree when with full force he pushed me. I couldn't stop myself from falling and as a result the tree and I went tumbling to the ground. The decorations were a complete mess and I was in the middle of it all. Steve just laughed and walked off still pretending to be in a playful mood. Leaving me feeling stupid and emotionally hurt. I remember the first thing I did after picking myself up was to pick the tree up and re decorate it. If any one had called the last thing I wanted was for them to see my house in a mess. I always felt if my house was clean and tidy everyone that visited would think my life was clean and tidy too. The mind has so many coping mechanisms. It was a way of hiding what was going on in my life to family and friends.

Steve would also do other random things to me. One evening we popped to our local pub for a quick drink. We argued for most of the evening. With each drink I felt a little braver and tried to address the problems we were having. It didn't work though. As we walked the short distance home we passed a hedge that led up to the path near my house. Without warning Steve gave me a huge shove. I fell sideways into the prickly hedge. My hands and face were cut. He thought it was hilarious. I can't really tell you why Steve did all of these things to me I can only surmise. When we met I was the one with the great job, lovely house and a dad that in Steve's eyes had money.

I think Steve saw me as an escape from his own life. He opened council toilets, he had a child at sixteen with his ex girlfriend and had no particular goals or aims in life.

I was his easy route to money. He was right. He bled me dry financially. Unfortunately in the process he bled me dry of my self esteem, confidence and self worth. It was never me as a person he was interested in, only what he could get from me.

I'm glad to say people like that never win in the end....

MY VALENTINE

Fifteen...

Ahhh...Valentine's day! This is a day to celebrate love. I don't remember any of the Valentine's days in our relationship being romantic really. Personally I'm a romantic and I tried to give romantic gestures on each of our valentine's days. I baked a heart shaped chocolate cake for our first valentine's day and thought it would look nice if I cut it into a broken heart shape. So I zigzagged a cut through the middle and decorated it. I didn't realise at the time the significance of doing this. I look back now and laugh at the irony of what I did.

Valentine's day also fell a week after the birth of our first son and as I had stitches after the birth I couldn't walk without a lot of discomfort so I didn't feel up to going out to buy anything. Instead I adorned the front room walls with silver heart shapes that I had made from silver foil. I thought this a lovely gesture but Steve wasn't impressed and actually criticised me for not buying him anything that year. Anyway one Valentine's day in particular is etched in my mind and will be for ever. I was pregnant with our second child and this particular Valentine's day fell on a Saturday. Oh joy!

I had been having bracksten hicks' pains (pains that lead up to labour) for a week or so but like all women, after a while I had gotten used to them and just carried on. However on Saturday 14th February 1998, at approximately four in the morning I was woken with an almighty shooting pain. I knew this was the start of my labour. I lay awake until my son woke up and then clambered out of bed to start my day as usual. Not long after, Steve got up and started getting himself ready to leave the house for his football match. I told him about the labour pain I had in the early hours and asked him not to go to his match. He refused to stay in with me and our son, however he was happy enough to drive us to my dad's house go to his football match then pick us both up straight after. My pains were very far apart and I knew it could be a while until they started to get closer together but I wasn't happy about Steve's decision to leave me to cope on my own. I wanted to be at home but decided being with my dad would be a better option than being at home on my own.

I arrived at my dads about midday and as the afternoon progressed so did my labour. My afternoon was spent running around after my two year old son who seemed to be particularly clingy that day. I remember praying to myself for Steve to come and pick us up soon. My dad was growing more and more concerned about me but didn't really know what to do. You can imagine my relief when Steve pulled up outside. It was about six o'clock at this point and my contractions were about fifteen minutes apart and very painful. After we had bundled Daniel and all his things into the car we set off. I relayed my painful afternoon to Steve and suggested we should ring his mum to look after Daniel while we went to the hospital. As I was talking I didn't really take too much notice of the route he was taking until we were close to the pub he frequented. "Where are we going?" I asked nervously. "I just want to go for a couple of pints!" he replied. "No, please?" I said, with tears in my eyes. "I can't drive home!" "Please?" I begged. He was not listening to me. He pulled up outside the pub and before I had a chance to say anything else he was out of the car and half way across the road. I could not believe what he had done. I was in tears and had no confidence or will to go into the pub and get him. Very painfully and slowly I got into the driver's seat and pulled off. The journey home meant I had to drive on the motorway for a few junctions but I thought that was the better option rather than the side roads.

It took about fifteen minutes to get home in which time my contractions were coming closer together. I was so scared but through the tears and the pain I knew I had to concentrate to make sure Daniel arrived home safely. The moment I had my son safely in the house I rang Steve's mother. It did not take long after I had explained what her son had done for her to drive to the pub where he was enjoying his pint. She dragged him out and home where he should have been all along. Like a puppy dog that had been slapped across the head he walked through the front door. He looked pathetic. The moment he looked at me I wanted to hurl myself at him and slap his sorry face, however in the state I was in that wasn't going to happen. Steve drove us to the hospital where I was placed on the maternity ward and looked after like I was actually human. Finally I felt safe and my mind could relax and let my body take over to do the job it was meant to do at that time. Jamie was born at 3.20 am 15th February 1998 and he was beautiful.

Valentine's day was forgotten! I now had another child that I needed to concentrate on. Out of such a terrible relationship two beautiful children were born. I suppose you could say they were the silver lining in my dark cloud....

94

REMEMBER, REMEMBER THE 5th OF NOVEMBER

Sixteen...

For a long time life turned into what felt like a daze. I was in a rut and it felt like life would never get any better for me. Each week the same, a repeat of the last. I had nothing to look forward to and nothing but heartache to look back on. Little did I know that things were about to change forever.

The 5th November 2000 began as normal. However it was the end of the day that was to throw me into a completely new way of life and one that took me nearly three years to pick myself up from. This particular morning I was feeling quite excited. I had booked tickets for a fireworks display hoping that this would be a nice surprise for Steve and the boys. We rarely did anything as a family and as the boys were at an age where their awareness was high I wanted them to start building nice memories. I remember the fireworks displays I was taken to as a child and I was hoping the boys would remember things we did with them as well. I smiled to myself all day. I had a definite spring in my step and I was feeling like I was going to start changing what we did as a family. I wanted to try and make life better for us. I suppose I was hoping this would be the catalyst to a new start for me and Steve. I can honestly say that despite everything that happened in our relationship I did love him although I'm sure you find that very hard to believe. When I was younger I always thought if I ever married it would be forever. I had never experienced troubles in my parents' marriage or my grandparents' marriage and I thought the person you married was the person you spent the rest of your life with. I thought marriage was sacred and that you should always try to make the best of what you had. I can understand if you think that sounds like madness after reading the experiences I had throughout my life with Steve, but it's true. I always hoped he would grow up and become the man I thought he should be. Anyway I digress!

I had walked Daniel to school and walked back home with Jamie who was now two. I wanted to get on with the house work and make the house spotless before we went out that evening. A clean home always made me feel in control. The day zoomed by and it was soon time to collect Daniel from school. While we walked home I explained to the boys where we were going that evening and they were so excited. I told the boys we were going to surprise daddy with the tickets when he arrived home from work and that seemed to excite them even more. I bathed and changed the boys and made sure they were fed before Steve arrived home so we could be on our way as soon as he was ready. He was late that evening. We waited and waited and finally he pulled up in the car port at the back of the house in his lorry. As soon as he walked through the gate the boys ran as fast as they could to see him. Excited jumbled words about tickets and fireworks spurting from their mouths. Steve looked at me confused. I explained about the tickets and the surprise evening. "Oh" he said quite underwhelmed. He walked into the house and went upstairs without saying anything else. I was a bit confused at his reaction but thought he was going upstairs to get washed and changed so I carried on sorting the boy out. When Steve finally came back downstairs he was indeed washed and changed and ready to go. Ready to go quite literally! Steve stood by the front door clean and smart with his kit bag over his shoulder. Quietly, soberly and with tears in his eyes he announced he was leaving. That was it! Nothing else. No fight, no shouting, no argument just a quiet declaration. I stood silent for what seemed like an age but was just a few seconds. "What?" "Why?" I stammered. Honestly over the years I had wished for this day to come but never envisaged it to be such a calm moment. Tears welled up in my eyes and I broke down. Steve just walked out of the front door and closed it behind him. I didn't really know what to do, I had screamed at him to go on countless occasions but I could never get rid of him. After all that time it was him that decided he was leaving. Again I suppose it was a control thing.

The boys were running around still excited to see the fireworks. They had not realised what had just happened. I don't know where I mustered the strength from but I slowly walked upstairs and splashed cold water on my face, brushed my hair and re applied my mascara. I walked back downstairs, put my coat on, gathered up what I needed for the boys and put them in the car. It was dark and raining but I was dammed if I was going to let my children down. We were going to see the fireworks! I managed to get to the display just as the fireworks were being set off. I stood right at the back of the field with Daniel in my arms and Jamie in his pram. With tears streaming down my face I watched the display for a while then, with two tired and cold children, I made my way back to the car. The three of us didn't really enjoy the fireworks. The boys were scared of the bangs and I had my mind on other things. I drove home in a bit of a daze and put the boys to bed then calmly poured myself a glass of wine.

My marriage had finally ended. Quite ironically really. All the years I had been with Steve my life was steeped in fireworks, metaphorically speaking of course. The end of an era had come and to finish it was a real fireworks display. Quite apt I suppose....

I THOUGHT IT WAS ALL OVER ... IT IS NOW

Seventeen...

So there it was, the end of my marriage. The end of all the hurt, the end of any more abuse. Well, not quite and in a way this was to be the hardest part of my relationship with Steve. My relief, happiness and ability to move on would have to wait. Why? Well, because of Steve of course.

If I'm honest our relationship was over well before he decided to walk out and call it a day. I could not stand to have him near me. I would physically tense up and go cold at his touch. Not only because of everything he had put me through over the years. Not only because of all the lies that had flooded from his mouth but there was yet another reason for my coldness. You see not long before he told me the marriage was over I had seen some hurtful text messages on his works mobile. (For those of you that don't know mobile phones were quite an oddity at this time; not the slim phones we know today but quite cumbersome objects.) I was cleaning the kitchen one evening after the boys had gone to bed.

Steve had gone out so I always tried to keep myself busy. It stopped me thinking too much. As I put things away I noticed his work's phone balancing on the edge of the kitchen cupboard. I took it down and just couldn't help myself. I looked at his messages and what I saw was just the icing on top of the mouldy, worm ridden cake we called a marriage. I think you have guessed! There were messages from another woman. Messages that could only lead me to believe that my husband was having an affair. I would like to say that I couldn't believe it but I could. In fact I had my suspicions for a while. Everything I had thought had been confirmed. I had accused him time and time again of seeing another woman. Well any wife would if their husband spent every weekend away from his family. He always denied it to the hilt of course. I think his mantra was deny, deny, deny! I don't remember crying, but I do remember a curtain of anger drop through my body. By the tone of the messages this wasn't something that had just started. It had obviously been going on for some time. This is what had driven him eventually to end the marriage. I should have been grateful. She really didn't know what she was getting herself into. I didn't look at it like that at the time though.

As I suggested at the beginning of this chapter the mental abuse continued for me even though Steve had decided to start a new life with someone else. The abuse he continued to bestow on me is what drove me to be the strong woman I am today.

Even though he had walked out that fireworks night he very quickly decided he was not going to leave the house. A few days after he left me he turned up with puppy dog eyes asking if we could talk. I fell for it and let him back in. After that he just took up residence on my sofa. You see when we married I made the rash decision to add him to my mortgage. I know, I know I can hear you screaming at me! I just thought it was the right thing to do. He didn't contribute financially however, he knew he was going to receive a 'lump sum'.

For nearly two years I had to put up with him sleeping on my sofa or in the garage if I managed to lock him out. That is where he found an extremely valued photo of me and Howard from Take That! I met Take That in Paris before I met Steve on a girls' weekend. That was my most treasured possession. I had hidden it for all those years and Steve decided to dispose of it. I never saw it again. Most of the time I had no option but to let him sleep in the house. At this point in time I was working part time on a helpdesk. It was evening work so I needed Steve to look after our sons. That was the only contact he had with the boys. The moment I stepped back into the house he would step out. He had lost all sense of responsibility for our gorgeous boys. He was far more interested in getting drunk and acting as though he was a teenager again. He started dressing too young and I have to say I felt quite embarrassed for him at times. He looked ridiculous. The boys would cry every time he left the house sometimes they would both cling to his legs trying to pull him back as he walked out of the door. It was heart breaking. I was the one every evening that had to pick up the pieces of their tiny broken hearts. Even when he was with them he was miles away.

I remember receiving a phone call from him one evening whilst I was working. He had rang me to tell me my youngest son who was three at the time had climbed out of his bedroom window and was hanging on by his fingertips. Apparently he was goaded on by his older five year old brother. They had been left on their own playing in their bedroom whilst Steve was on the phone to his girlfriend and it turned out they were in the throws of booking a holiday together. So while he was pretending that he had money to burn and tried to impress her, one of his children was in danger. It was Daniel's screams that made him wander upstairs to find his youngest son in that dangerous predicament. That scared him enough to call me and I was home in a flash to try and calm the situation down.

Another time he had left some presents in the kitchen for me. Communication had broken down completely between us by this point and I was happiest when he was not in the house. What I found this particular evening however broke my heart when I realised how little he thought of his children at this point. Can I ask you to think for a second, ask yourself how you would feel if you found drugs in your kitchen left there by someone you thought would know better. Pretty shocked and saddened I'm guessing. That's one thing but a completely different feeling when you realise they are in grasping distance of your children. Just think of the consequences! Well, that's what he had done. He had left small e-tabs sitting on the edge of the kitchen counter. I wasn't sure what they were at first but had my suspicions. I could not believe it. Immediately I felt the blood drain from my face. I threw them down the sink with thoughts of what could have happened if one of my children had grabbed hold of them. I felt sick. I turned and leant on the work surface for a while and stared into space for a few seconds. When my eyes focused again I noticed a video tape leaning up against the kettle. I picked it up wondering what it was. There was nothing written on the side or the front of this tape and I had never seen it before. Tentatively I walked to the front room and ushered the boys into the back room for a while where most of their toys were. I closed the living room door and put the tape into the recorder. You have probably guessed what it was already. Yes, a pornographic film. My reaction was one of disgust. Within seconds I had pulled the tape out of the machine and ripped the tape from the cartridge. It seemed to me that was what his life was about at this point, sex and drugs! I was living a nightmare. My estranged or should that be 'strange' husband was sleeping on the sofa when he wasn't sleeping elsewhere. He taunted me with his girlfriend, booked holidays and still thought it was his right to put me down as often as he could. His mission was basically to stop me having a life of my own. Not once did he offer to look after the boys so I could have an hour or so to myself. I was shattered physically and emotionally with it all. I cried myself to sleep most nights and that was in between either of the boys waking in the night. Finally I'd had enough. Out of the blue I gained the strength to visit a solicitor and started divorce proceedings. It was the best thing I had ever done. It gave me a feeling that I had never felt before. **Empowerment!** What a fantastic feeling!

I suddenly realised I had the law on my side and it opened up a new world to me. I could finally make Steve leave the house. I suddenly felt like I could do anything. It wasn't long after that I found a babysitter. This meant I didn't need Steve at all anymore. You see I had asked him on countless occasions to look after our sons so I could go out but he refused every time. He knew there was a possibility of me meeting someone and he was not about to let that happen. He still wanted to control me even though he was with his girlfriend every night. I decided to take control so I put a few leaflets through my neighbour's doors and along came Joanne. She baby-sat every Wednesday evening and I turned that into my night out with a friend I had lost touch with over the years. I'm glad to say our friendship withstood the years apart and we picked up right where we had left off. I also started to look for full time work and within a few weeks I was back working for a stationery company with colleagues I worked with at the time I met Steve. Life seemed to turn around for me in an instant and I was the happiest I had ever been. Working, taking care of my children without the help of their dad both financially and physically and having a social life for the first time in eight years. I felt like I could take on the world and I did.

Steve did not like the new me at all and tried on countless occasions to bring me back down but to no avail. He would stork me and creep into the house whilst I wasn't expecting him. Once whilst I was on the phone to a friend talking about a night out we had, he gave me the fright of my life. He had listened to my conversation until he heard something he didn't like. I had in fact had a fleeting kiss with a stranger and once he heard that he pounced on me. He pushed me about and when he realised it was not having the effect he was hoping for he launched himself at the living room door and punched a hole straight through it. I took control of the situation some how and managed to get him out of the house and lock the door. In tears I fell to the floor but within minutes I had picked myself back up and decided I was not going to let him make me feel scared anymore. I grew ten feet taller every time I won a battle with him. My confidence through working and socialising again slowly made me stronger. It took nearly three years from him saying he was leaving to me living happily and feeling content again. Steve had his payout from me and it was quite a considerable amount. He took it and oddly enough that was when he started to leave me alone.

It was then that I met someone new. Someone completely different from Steve. Someone who believed I could do whatever I wanted if I put my mind to it. Someone who loved my children like they were his own. This man gave me the space I needed to enjoy time with friends and eventually I'm very glad to say, Steve turned into a distant bad memory....

JUST ME... AND THERE ARE STILL THREE

Eighteen...

All that is left to do is to briefly let you know how everyone is to this day. Well I am now working in the pharmaceutical industry and have been for the past nine years. I set myself a goal, worked hard and took the exams needed to start in this competitive industry. Unfortunately my new relationship did not work out. However after a pretty great five year relationship and one gorgeous daughter later, we amicably came to the end of the road. I have my own home and live happily with the three people I love and care for the most.

The boys are wonderful, handsome well adjusted young men who are forming great futures for themselves by doing things they love the most. They now have a great relationship with their dad and I always encourage them to see him as often as they want to. I don't know if he has changed and have no need or want to find out. As long as my sons' are happy then I am too! I have nothing to do with their dad and find that to be the best way forward in my life. My little girl is a happy, clever and independant five year old. She is five going on ten! My wish to write about the horrendous experiences I had all those years ago has now finally been realised. My hope is that it has helped you understand a little bit about what an abusive relationship looks like from the inside. I also hope that reading my stories has helped you understand why sometimes these relationships go on for years. In a nutshell I would say it is fear that stops either party from moving on. Fear of people finding out what has been happening and fear of the unknown outside the relationship. Fear of what will happen if you say you are leaving. Everything about ending the relationship is scary and the fear of being a failure. I think there is someone for everyone out there. It just takes longer for some to find that perfect person. In the process of life and the need to share our lives with someone we can sometimes end up meeting the wrong person.

You are probably wondering what my thoughts are on men right now. I have to say I do have very high standards and a lot of tick boxes that I look for in a man and on that note that is probably why I am still single. I remember reading a fridge magnet on one of my friend's fridges one day. It read "Love like you have never been hurt!" Think about that statement for a second! We all do that don't we? When we meet someone new we tend to be open to what that new person can offer. I'm no different, however I think we should all have a minimum standard. Shall I just say I am enjoying my single life, I'm having fun and working hard to make life even better for me and my children. In the process I have met Mr for now, Mr maybe and even Mr WOW, wish you were mine! Ha-ha, whilst all the while knowing deep down that Mr right will more than likely find me.

Life is for living not putting up with and there is only one person that can make life great. Yes! You guessed it. It's you! You are the one person responsible for you. So look after yourself. We have one life so live it well!

I wish you all a great life. ✗ ✗ ✗ ✗

NO LIFE ALOUD!

Short stories depicting true life experiences.

Delve into an abusive relationship. Read about it from a perspective within four walls. Do you know anyone in a similar situation? I bet you do! You probably just don't realise it because the abused will never tell you. I want you to know although I tell 'my story' I could also be writing about many, many other abusive relationships.

I want the positiveness to shine through and help you recognise manipulative behaviour patterns. Also I want to show you some small and some not so small abusive acts that happen without anyone realising.

My account is written from the heart with the hope I can help others in similar or worse situations. Life can be hard! Sometimes it feels as though there is no end to your problems. I want you to realise there is light at the end of the tunnel. Once you realise there is one person in your life with the strength and ability to make your life better, you will fly in life. That person is of course, YOU!

Life is for living not putting up with. Dig in, find your inner strength and make your life better.... I have!

I wish you a great life..... *X X X X*

NO LIFE ALOUD!

Short stories depicting true life experiences.

Delve into an abusive relationship. Read about it from a perspective within four walls. Do you know anyone in a similar situation? I bet you do! You probably just don't realise it because the abused will never tell you. I want you to know although I tell 'my story' I could also be writing about many, many other abusive relationships.

I want the positiveness to shine through and help you recognise manipulative behaviour patterns. Also I want to show you some small and some not so small abusive acts that happen without anyone realising.

My account is written from the heart with the hope I can help others in similar or worse situations. Life can be hard! Sometimes it feels as though there is no end to your problems. I want you to realise there is light at the end of the tunnel. Once you realise there is one person in your life with the strength and ability to make your life better, you will fly in life. That person is of course, YOU!

Life is for living not putting up with. Dig in, find your inner strength and make your life better.... I have!

ISBN 978-0-9928369-0-0

I wish you a great life.....
        X X X X X X

9 780992 836900 >

CPSIA information can be obtained at www.ICGtesting.com
Printed in the USA
LVOW04s1633060715

445137LV00020B/1334/P